T0136438

M A N D E R L E Y

MANDERLEY

Poems by Rebecca Wolff

UNIVERSITY OF ILLINOIS PRESS

Urbana and Chicago

Grateful acknowledgment to *BOMB, Colorado Review, Columbia: A Journal of Literature and Art, Exquisite Corpse, Grand Street, Iowa Review, Open City, Paris Review, Provincetown Arts, Southern Poetry Review, Western Humanities Review.*

© 2001 by Rebecca Wolff
All rights reserved

∞ This book is printed on acid-free paper.

Library of Congress Cataloging-in-Publication Data
Wolff, Rebecca, 1967–
Manderley : poems / by Rebecca Wolff.
p.   cm. — (National poetry series)
ISBN 0–252–02698–5 (cloth : alk. paper)
ISBN 0–252–07005–4 (paper : alk. paper)
I. Title. II. Series.
PS3623.O56M3   2001
811'.6 — dc21   2001001515

THE NATIONAL POETRY SERIES

The National Poetry Series was established in 1978 to ensure the publication of five poetry books annually through participating publishers. Publication is funded by the late James A. Michener, the Copernicus Society of America, Edward J. Piszek, the Lannan Foundation, the National Endowment for the Arts, and the Tiny Tiger Foundation.

2000 COMPETITION WINNERS

Jean Donnelly of Washington, D.C., *Anthem*
Selected by Charles Bernstein, published by
Sun & Moon Press

Susan Atefat Peckham of Michigan, *That Kind of Sleep*
Selected by Victor Hernández Cruz, published by
Coffee House Press

Spencer Short of Iowa, *Tremolo*
Selected by Billy Collins, published by
HarperCollins Publishers

Rebecca Wolff of New York, *Manderley*
Selected by Robert Pinsky, published by the
University of Illinois Press

Susan Wood of Texas, *Asunder*
Selected by Garrett Hongo, published by
Viking Penguin

To my relations

The house was a sepulchre, our fear and suffering lay

buried in the ruins. There would be no resurrection.

When I thought of Manderley in my waking hours

I would not be bitter. I should think of it as it might

have been, could I have lived there without fear.

I should remember the rose-garden in summer,

and the birds that sang at dawn. Tea under the

chestnut tree, and the murmur of the sea

coming up to us from the lawns below.

—DAPHNE DU MAURIER, *REBECCA*

CONTENTS

MANDERLEY

Occasional Poem
for the Fairchilds

Nobody lives in your sleep.
Not in the dream you dream, for all your selves
are represented in your dreaming, every character
is you and you are too.
We are a flock.

And in your family
you are everyone
though now we dream of emigrating
out of there. Maybe you all need
each other now.

Perhaps we kept her here. No one dies in your sleep,
there is a rumor that if we dream
of dying we do die. And if she died

in their sleep then no one is the worse
for passing in and out of states
of rest, and love's transition is from pasture
to pasture.

The Royal Begonia

She stole soil from the royal gardens
on her visit to the castle
and found it pleasant, while it rained,
to sit on the bench between the rows
of glistening darlings—
front to the exotics, back to the domestics—
the exotics all of a species
that looked like a feather duster.

She spoke to the gardener himself,
as he planted signs in the blistering order,
in the downpour that excluded
so much even while it pumped
its blood into the display.
She followed his path,
and in front of the bed whose load
of earth she'd lightened
she came close,
out of some noblesse oblige,
or politesse,
to telling him of the liberty
she'd taken. But then thought better
of it—thought instead sentimentally

of the waving begonia,
maturing in parti-colored splendor
on her sooty windowsill, pleasuring bees
and the sun and the nearby candlestick
alike. And then she chatted blindly
of the path she'd taken in her life,
up to this day, and surreptitiously
kicked the royal earth with her royal toe.

Tunnel Visionary

Dead men dangling
and lying everywhere. The rhododendrons
are fecund as gangrene—
rhododendrons not in flower
but in redundancy.
The path was frightening all along,
I had to stop writing, in the light rain
the ink was running, the promissory sky
reneging, remaining absolutely gray.
In crowds of trees I see, between
the trees, an awesome
thicket, so dark green and above
all still. Too full and carved.
This tableau is virgin;
it has not held a step
since one was murdered last. I know a body
was perfectly discovered,
I know it decomposed
fast in that crèche of mulch.
I see its whole form now, but leave off
horror as I leave off
omniscience sometimes.
Walking, my theorem runs:

if history is a tunnel,
timed ribs supporting a structure,
then it is collapsible
like a traveling-cup.
Chuckling, walking.
That I could believe it to be so!
Unpinioned forms of simultaneity
lodged at all times (face down
in the moss or floating
in shallow foam at pond's edge).
But it is the farfetched day now,
it all happened, and it's happening
in my sight. Leaf upon leaf, in captivity,

I see bodies in the way every insult
loosed has a voice
like thought. A veil as thin
as smoke from cooking tells
the king what crime is possible
to say. And the spooky rhododendrons
grow analogous up and over, weaving
darkness from daylight in kudzu-like
fever to enslave.

Broads Abroad:
Elizabeth Bishop & Jane Bowles

Approaching the subject in a gamine,
in a fey way. Elfin, nicely sloshed
with the reticence of the foreign, they knew some
of the same faggots in New York. She had
one square husband: fey, *gamin,* not without
the shallow, tyrannical self-consciousness that might produce
an existentialist classic. Men in the role of dead papa. The basic
subject that of experience in question, they took
it overseas to rest—phobic, unable to breathe or swallow
scenes presented to the offended sense
of delinquence. Not tickled by the locals
but enslaved. Mops on top, they make good
lives, you see, because the lives they lived
typify a rotten core. Presented as fermented,
a hapless party-girl deduction based on artsy-fartsy
from the word "go." Something gravitated naively
toward the ones they loved. *In exile you just keep drinking*
and thinking about birds and flowers: the little monkeys
with their big hands inhabit you. Un moue *for the record.* Detail
informing your countrymen of the importance of your contribution. Agog
in the arms of a native woman your hair flops
madly, radiant with henna. Deck-chair Madonna
in a practiced way, never in a family way,
musking over jailbait, just as good as you knew how to be,
dried up nicely now and fuming with detection.

Couched

as in cloaked. Made with little marks
describing arcs and boots, feet
inside their hearts

rescue immanent, subservient
no longer to the dominant
parachute. Material hot air

braving personality, given
reason to believe that we are whole
again at last sustaining

the blows we have subsisted
on. Time for a question: do you love
her? (hold or be held) You certainly come

at the thought
with a vengeance. And nothing
will get you famous

quicker than a parade
of values. Belts
and buckles

long in the face
of a long separation. Action preempts
so very much. Time to cry out.

He wrapped himself in my warmest . . .

On the subway (gun to temple) individual
action rising out of individual desperation.
He closed the door. A Christmas tree wrapped in its own shroud
on New Year's Day defaming the shade
it casts, terror's decoy on the macabre walk
home through the clement streets where celebrants are done
exhausting my city. There is only so much to incite in a mass
of the oppressed behind the scenes. I stroll down the avenue in need
of a bigger space inside the space provided, between
the outside of the inner perimeter and the buffer on the inside
of the outer: *this dream.* A crow flew,
a flat plane was built up on a ravaged purity. Unknowable,
unspeakable trinkets were offered to the caveman. In exchange,
rapid transit. I finally saw what it all looked like before I got here.
Everyone I see is "in the theatre," is the abominable androgyne,
not merely lapsed but a link, never before missed: one hand
outstretched to the blessed, cursed outcome, one
to the progenitors, and one thrust down
the front of his/her dashing jeans. Do you see any spoils? A handheld
camera trained on the glorious grainy documentation of what's trashed,
          portraying
himself in a flash of silver lamé. I grow to hate my age. He could never fake
responsibility but he can make me come now, to the realization.
Feathers dropping out of a blue sky over the reservation,
incidentally faster in the warm rain, a cop outside the cigar store
on the corner spins on a dime to apprehend a noisemaker.

Spending the Day on a Sleeping Porch

This is the enclosure my family
has dreamed of, and brought into being
by the sheer collected force of our dreaming:
a fund. Generations of desire for repose, after chatting
away the seamless day in recalling
our forefathers and, separately, their sins: mistresses,
the oppressions perpetrated on those who were loyal
and lived behind the house. We are
not even midway through yet.

There is something radical about doing this.
Check the action for resonance:
blue planks create a platform;
there is a sense that something will be performed
in this flimsy envelope. "Don't follow me"
is the general cry.
My mom feels that way.
By the close of the reunion day
she is ready to be shorn of all relation.
Uncle Pete is of a
mind: he is ready for his body to hit
the traditional burnpile; to ash up with paper plates and cups
and blow away in the cool
breeze, the breeze much commented on.

But nothing in the lineage of this house
expresses how I feel about the sleeping porch.
It provides an elegant barrier,
tightly woven of vision: from inside, I can see,
but cannot be seen by, the involuntary squadron
of my genealogy, with their clanking
chains and requisite pedigree.
Never mind the leafy branch of the magnolia tree
that reaches almost all the way now
to the ground. This is the only place
in the house not overrun
by familiars: the family
cat, dog, resemblance . . .
It is outside the house though quite partial to it,
as Aunt Nell was in her day to barbecue.
It offers simulacra to the breeze.

It is a room built for continuity, with one wall
and three veils. Here I have observed that
you must indeed follow children around,
endlessly, or they will kill themselves
at every opportunity.

I liked it so much he gave it to me as a present

Freud's letters freight the nightstand, a tacit
rejoinder. I dream pure hysteria:
vines writhing, porthole of wisteria
through which to view pale reason's dense mandate.
Zoom in on mother's nipple, latent
closeup. Real content is mystery—a
girl's dark skull swivels: *Suspiria,*
Italian frightfest, young TV's nascent
bosom. Some kind of matriarchal code—
worms mapping out a nest of lingerie—
tells me the bloom is off the rose, the road
to sense, translation, to the NEA
"restructured" as in old Russia. Crude mode
of *rapprochement,* badly dubbed DNA.

Mom gets laid

in all manner of positions
promising and compromising
and uncompromising. Under ferns,
in glades. Downstream, upwind.
Talk about transgression . . .

this one has a huge cock.
This one takes a finger up the ass to make
him come. Her injunction is to have fun
at the expense of anyone.

Verboten, the extravagant
gesture of attachment. "Where do people
get all those rules they use with each other?
'I could never love someone I didn't respect.' Bah! The finger puppet's
head just pops onto my fingertip." Says Mom.

Mom gets laid and then flies
down to Rio for a damaging abortion. Mom gets laid, flies
off the handle. In fright wig
and Jacuzzi Mom gets laid. You must never insist

she doesn't or your face will stick that way—grimacing
in snaggle-toothed derision—
for an eternity of multiple
cordialities. Shake hands with Mom's
bed-partner: get down

on your knees, for a change, and
take a workmanlike approach
to what is usually inspired. *Corn Cob, Lollipop,*

Undulating Stream.
Mom is not causality: Mom
is, in reverse, a woman bent
on dignifying her own comment
with reply. A mom

who makes the charmed world of desire
seem an economy. Who takes the calm
Lake of Requite between her thighs
and cracks the nut. Mom

is unidentifiable, unafraid;
the gadget heavy with ropes and chains
and buckles. She presses a shiny
allowance into my palm. A
complete concordance.

Mom sells me directly
into prostitution. Mom gets old
and loses her appeal. Mom,
I think, derives some satisfaction, in her dotage,

from my flexibility. Later,
she is a totem and stands, nipples
erect for all to see, singing
in a downpour in the rainforest.
Talk about transgressive . . .

"The king is dead!" I shrieked
from the fathoms of my fetal doze. And
woke just in time. "Then I am the King
of the Cats!" Mom cried and jumped

up from the table and out
through the window. Leaving
the hearth no colder.

Flame On

Every time I approach this borrowed hearth I see the face
of the one I love. In the fire? No—maybe
in the log, on fire? Or is it in the action of the log,
thrown into the fire, that I briefly catch a glimpse of his visage?
It's so romantic, kneeling here, I wonder why
I don't just stay all day. His whole body,
riddled with inference, stretching out atop
the fevered flames.

I walk to the fireplace in performance of a function,
in perpetuity. What is triggered
by noon—the sun, spreading over the ribs
of the room, defers its gloomy dominion—in the back
of the brain is an installation; a vision: a whole room
filled with observers—an audience—on site, glued
to the spectacle of me, returning once more, then again, to my spot
on the hearth, whence I throw a switch.
The light blazes on, electrified, conducive, evocative
motion of the mind. He just barely scratches the surface.

Don't know what to call him
but he's mighty lak a rose

It is a red wax candle
between us on the table. Lurid,
in decay. Do you want to make something
of it? It is melting,
slipping out pools of its own soft
heart: blood running under a door.
Somebody smells like honeysuckle, he says.
We have just enough wine tonight.
There are several liquids at this table;
his dewy eyes, clear white, bright blue.

It is round and sacrilegious,
squat, advantageous. And my friend is orgasmic,
always a distinction to be made. I never saw the like
before tonight, when I looked down from our chatter
and he stopped before I came. Don't give up on glamour,
it is apportioned: I am rolling a rose (in bloom) lipstick-true
out of the runoff. I hand it over to you
you are flirting your face off.
It is all so base, no matter how we
elevate it to the level of this object
this subject. If you are not your body and you are not your mind . . .
your beard knits your head and chest together. Others subject
themselves at the outset, prostrated, and that is a prerequisite.
Just don't hurt me.

Motion Picture Adaptation

Moonlight. We have a body full
of engagement, en route to the Kingdom
Hall for a country evening's primal
distraction. "Some of us"—whispers my sister, cloaked
in muslin—"have no such need
for mollification: I would
remain intent on plying the handiwork
that recommends me—see?"
But the lamp gutters, under duress, casts little
light on our undoing inside
the vehicle. This oil that burns up blackness, vehicular,
gives in to motion's slick
demand: it sloshes, spatters; what coinage.

The attachments we have forming within
us presently may be the last we ever
glimpse by this deranged
moonglow. Soon, they have whispered, the century
will bring us constant clamor for our efforts, the
illuminated banging of luxury. "I, for one,
know when to hold my tongue, to distract ardor
with the blindness of my craft."
Transported from one great gaping
hole in the fabric
of our knowledge to another, we are reduced
by candlelight to girlish things: witticism
drawn from a small store of such
phrases as serve the day's purpose. We must be guided
by departed spirit. My sister

is rich in catechism, her response,
purely felt: "You'll never catch me feelingly
proclaiming false distinctions; a lover is a lover
and a prospect is prospective. If I set
my cap on conquest, then a lion's
what I'll snare."

A lion in England? I am unmoved.
"Oh, to be sure. I can already hear his roar
when I unveil him in the lair."

Conquering Ambivalence

I didn't understand where all the feeling
flowed from. The fount of intention
hovering midair like a dirigible, its manifold
petals unfolding. For this deluge
of deferred sentiment, a perfect metaphor:

Ichabod Crane. You've been so much in my thoughts
and grown there. In hollow, in daft
intertextuality, you slept in the hollow
of my heart. In Sleepy Hollow, you know
she wakes after a hundred
years with a long beard when kissed
by your grace. Holding his head
under his arm. That and other dismemberments in concert.

Sleeping under a tree on moss
and moss making the difference; confronted
with a ghost or just feeling ghosted by a representative
figure acting as a repository for all the proscribed
and deeply felt. Under a tree for a hundred years
and awoken slowly, in keeping with a new capacity
for love's large gesture, to face the looming

mandible of surety, a sense of unholy
integration. The long beard was a clue to what
had been missing. The Prince. Charming decapitated,
only to be reconfigured more wholly as in . . . *O my love.*
These years have not been wasted but instead charged.
Sleeping and sleeping in a fugue, treed, before
waking to feel concerted, regrouped. How long did she sleep

before struggling to wake? Apology for the delay
coming in the form of speech garbled—gobbledygook—
in the ultralucid fashion
of the sleeper, who means just what it sounds like.

I'm putting all my eggs in one basket. With all
the solemnity and portentousness of a third-grade teacher,

of a third-rate preacher, I'm pouring all my energy
into the scene, the fabled glen, the nook, and two figures.
One asleep and waking, one decapitated, kissing.

Interminable Silence

These fakirs really know how to eat—
sit back on your haunches, put the book
away, every grain slides down your gullet
that much easier for the open passage
of time.

To emulate more closely
those chipmunks, clearly
at play, one dares the other to cross the road.
An astonishing display of free will
and volition. You must be

kidding. I haven't written a poem
in over a year. "Kinesthesia"
meant almost nothing to me before
today. And on this day I'll not assume to speak
for both of us. Can you imagine

Charles Dickens?
He must have lived in a dream, all day
every day, in the abattoir. It's pretty to be in the sun.
I'd like to think I could stay this side
of the hill forever, divining

my one true voice from all the others, including
rocks and shards of bone. I think
I could enlarge my life to include that.
I cannot imagine wishing to abduct
and assault the little blond girl

yet there she is, turnabout
fair play and whatever is in her heart
shall occupy mine. *Squeak   squeak*. Her tricycle breaks
down and off she goes
inside to mom for cosseting.

Letters, Young and Old Poets

Truro
Nov. 29

And when you despaired, what sustained you?

. . . . .

Directed. Directive: you ask. I am a slow
learner. Coming around corners the dilemma,
a shrinking light they put before me.
A melodrama when I tell you half.
The edge of the seat thing: nausea in the lap of memory,
presently a soft look comes over me.

Today is someone's birthday.
On this day I do nothing to hurt
anybody. Sites of exquisite communion
observed. The perfect word replaced. Oh spill the milk,

spill the milk again.
Vanity. Favoritism. Strong curtain
fluttering for rent. I must travel
far in excess. Back to the graveyard,

wreathed in smiles.
Such childbearing going on between these portals.
Remember the smell of a fairy ring crushed,
"Aux mortes." Toward grass
and any young rabbit crushed in it. Conspirators,
I just heard of *duende.* Oh give me a home . . .

· · · · ·

Sagres
April 24th

Do you really? I can't feel it.

· · · · ·

Nothing came to replace the devil
in my heart. A paltry vivacity.
Even in my weakened state
I change this place. Clumsy, lurching,
like a monster. But like a monster I'm working
my way toward you. I will not whore myself.
There is actually nothing wrong with me.
The smell of paint saves it. Industry,
slapping something white on the old wall.

· · · · ·

Glasgow
Tuesday the 25th

Who are these animals that I entertain?

· · · · ·

I could be alone when instead I am with them.
There were parts of me they liked. A quorum
compromising. Bald statement, everything so easeful
it erases its

Back to not understanding. Rich,
the story of my phantom containment: a small,
modernized garret.

I sleep well in the colder air.
Memories of the seminary—any tight space.

. . . . .

Roma
Wednesday, November 26th

Darling, sweetheart. When?

. . . . .

Trust a reconstructed mind to resist
the impulse. One is surviving when
resisting. Swallowing
in immature silence.

Weather on top.
Stupid, but not evil,
inside and outside, in the service.
Events appear to conspire.
A struggle to keep up my end.

Spring forward, fall back

These particular urns are so generous
and when we deliver to ourselves—
and ourselves to—the square field
in the morning we are plenty itself! Cashing in.

They have pushed aside the tall grasses for us
in either direction. I cannot
walk beside you, Mr. Contingency; we hop from rock
to rock over the marshy bits, a score
composing itself: Here is where the skin is nicked on a capsized trunk.
Repeatedly the lazy deer has fallen short of its desires.

I love clearings because they are so open. By saying
love we can resist the temptation to qualify.
The year's fallen leaves have aspired to this monochrome rapture.
The grass in the clearing so green; the clearing
more capacious even than "meadow."

Oceans, mountaintops, significant
holdings receive an allotment of our damage.
One clearing away, tumultuous resentments
and specific preferences happen upon that spot
where the sun displays itself
with hormonal force—like when a man can no longer pretend

to be either self-possessed or embarrassed. Hence the randy libretto: "Oh fuck me, sun, fuck me."

In the clearing in the green the element of surprise

and our camouflage resists distinction.

The Lowest Common Denominator

This is paradise. Sitting in the hot sun,
idolized. It's a Montessori school: the kids
fly like darts in their neon sheaths
from the school bus into the heart of the waiting
parent, parked on the shoulder in a steaming
pickup. Foggy Spring. Humid in a brilliant wash
of past, sea nearby. A wizened, essentialist

paradigm: *if you are happy:* impression of the new moon in first
quarter, first day of spring, a fungus grown
on the regressive azure sky: *I am happy.* It's an all-ages
hardcore show. Broadcast tiny seeds,
slowing the utterance to a standstill
in perpetual oxymoron: "'Self-consciousness.' It's come
to mean embarrassed . . . ill at ease."
My personal sphere including a matched set of advanced

communications concepts. Talking with:
software interface designer Nick,
28. We will bring our friend-
ship limping into the 21st
century. *He was relieved to discover,*
after all these encoded years, that I could hold up
my end of a conversation
about intelligence, in which we (restraining ourselves) *touched on*
art, and life, the possibilities (so limited and so dated,
in the predawn light)

of communication. In this era. That's his job. Many bitter
failures of the will later, still

there is a unit of information
to be wished on and blown away: "my personal bliss
on a day like today." His hair came alive for me today. How much
of my flooded, muddy body will fit
in the memory? We will find, if not a language,
a series of stabs at it, like unearthing old gold in the yard

rolled into tubes like subway tokens. It is a local
produce farmstand steaming in the first sun, early morning,
losing its dew. *When you are happy:*

Firefly

We have opened up an establishment
by the side of the road. Occupying
an abandoned position, a foregone
conclusion; twice-told, foreclosed.
We hope to make good use of a space
that was poignant for its cultural
insignificance, an eyesore

from bygone days of absolute
value. What was here was non-
transferable; they served up pie
and coffee. We offer a menu
of inexhaustible delicacy: one dish collected
from the surfeit of each blasted country, arranged carefully
on the surface so as not to displease the eye
in synchronicity with its mother
tongue. Again we have that feeling

"I do everything,
and it's relatively rewarding." Picture
statuettes and friezes, a well-trained
gauntlet of discrete professionals, glacial
chill preserving water at its highest
arc: it tumbles from the fountain's throat
like a goat skittering down a hillside. And feast
your eyes on Firefly.

The restaurant is ominously busy.
It makes a noise. And like everything, this
venture acquires its significance
through a process similar
to investment. *I feel so clean and tired all the time.*
I am here working like a god
—excuse me,
like a dog. Slow—
embarrassingly so—
the movement of the hand
after the eye, in going
to swat the unlit fly
in the light of day

and as any relationship is unequal
inasmuch as it is forged—the doubled,
quartered
symmetries of a winged miscreant,
a man and woman dancing
around and around an erection—
so will be this partnership
of parts.

"What kind of an establishment is this?!"
—indignant voices
 rising above the genial hum
 of the general throng
"Congratulations," I shrieked,
"that is absolutely beautiful.
It is not often, after all, that you will find
the maker at his center."

        . . . . .

For one thoughtless moment I
identified myself with a pale moth
trapped inside at closing time. I opened
a file at random and came to a happy
coincidence, a correspondence: recollected
in tranquility, the most beautiful word ever spoken
or written (of course,
in English): file it under
Firefly. And fix your eyes
upon the object of which Desire has chosen to make

its reproduction. It must be so much fun:
concept and execution. There is a staircase
on the property, which we do ascend. The floor—we decided
for the floor on a sea-water green. It very nearly reminds me
of the ocean, waving,
on and on, on and on. A customer once said to me:
"I can't go drowning in the sea
(*at the end of my life*)
without seeing a lot of these tiny white lights."
—"Congratulations," I shrieked . . .

"Once you have settled on an image
to be reproduced
allegorically
it will be replicated
ad infinitum. And
in this roundabout way
you will discover
the many ways
in which there is always
one within the . . ." If this were a museum

we would have to ask you constantly to still
your tapping toes, hush
your jubilant cries. As it is, feast
your eyes. Clarity is
in the domain of the beholden.
We offer this special
honeymoon rate, no
guarantee of ascension—a getaway
from the tyranny of the emotion.
And again we have that feeling

of *something's gotta give*
We'll make a go of it.

Objects of formal beauty
won't you shine your light at least
until the firefly—
        by firelight
        is extinguished.

The world is my cloister

Last night I sliced the tip of my thumb off—again,
I'm all thumb.
Until it comes to its fruition
it upsets me
I saw the gap and it was scary—

that's the lingo
for come and comfort me.
The ingrates struggle

with so much candor.

· · · · ·

Is it not meet
that you should make of my home a home
for you and yours? It transforms unduly the deck, the flower
garden, the peach
tree, my god, the peach tree becomes
you. You have grown to reach its height
and are never alone now, in due process. The cat beats
her tail in time with your attention, your two
feet extend off the edge of the bed. At home

last night I dreamt I went to Manderley again.

It's just a nightmare, the loss of love—
someone with one foot
makes more than one noise walking
across the brick. Damn that which resists
articulation, damn everything so like.
Looking at pictures,
dwelling in the particulate
separation of flesh from limb,
flesh from globe, gold
threshed away for sale at common market.

I have not spoken this way
for a long time, to anyone.
Now I stop speculating on the quality
of His love. It's realized.

· · · · ·

An obscure population
we must raise them
build a house foursquare
an exact replica of
the poetry "world." *Manderley.* We will take each other
seriously. That which does not kill us
blah blah blah. Bucksaw bucked across
a crackdown on imitation. A thousand projects
cut out for my

leisure. I can shake my head now, in disbelief
and rue. Rue, rue. Rue
the day gone by in circles
of deception. A millstone in the back unmoved
since Canaan, *plant*
my grave for me. Built of poplar to outsmart
termites, laid in at all angles, foursquare,
creating rooms that turn and twist
in the wind. They don't build citadels
like that anymore. A walled city involving
wasp's nests for insulation against springtime.
The winds did blow.
Told of youth.

          . . . . .

And when the master comes downstairs
I pretend to pick at my food. Pleasure's problem
is its wordlessness. "Something is awry"
is all he has to say. "Oh, do
as I do, do as I do," my
reply. I stay in position. He keeps me. Riddled with imitators,
I am taking my good fortune
in stride. End of identity.
Immense reserves of tenderness

. . . in which a joke falls flat. *End of riddle.*

Constant in Opal

No one has gotten any older without
first making this kind of gesture, in which
one's pain takes its own measure,
like a diabetic callously pricking
her stalwart thumb to check for sugar. No one says shit
about bad luck anymore for fear
it will come knocking at the front
or back door. Like a piece of fortune.

> *Like a parsed-out sentence.*
> *Like a big whore passed out in your arms.*
> *Like a trace of the lively disjunction you simply cannot afford.*

When you sit down to tell a story
to the ocean, your friend the ocean,
and you wax lyrical, and you make
the same dumb mistake over and over
again—you tell the only really bad joke over and over—
one consolation: your friend can never get up and leave
you. Like some other bodies of water will.

> *To be deserted by a continent, or an already*
> *vacant lot; what a truant*
> *desolation. What a load of poignant*
> *rot. I had already said*

When the music's over,
turn out the light, *but apparently it wasn't
enough;* Oh retarded dementia, just keep
away from me.

Please stay me at your door.
That's the plainest plea you'll ever hear from me.

Ashtabula County

1. *In Motion*

Black dog trapped on
the median. Endless
Caverns; touristic fabrication.
The more bucolic, the more disastrous—
the applicant can't tell—her aching muscles
stretch!—that every day from now on
will not be just like this.
Just exactly.

Tennessee Technological University.
The dean has given me the positive
reaction: "Thumbs up, yonder Christian!"—
I am emboldened to strike a pose
of heroism, feet on the clay
turned to grass, to asphalt. Shoulder
the arena of mobilization.

Consumer Education. I am not
who I thought I was again
and again. At this juncture
the board requests a reassessment: open wider,
over and over. To the mountain,
face the heavens, greet your maker
in the full regalia of your matter.
Tennessee Theological University:

if you go up it will be windier.
There is risk of damage. If you go down
the rivers may rise. Your vehicle
will not save you. The standard
that you hold yourself to you would
also hold the condition of our nation's
highways and byways.

2. *In Place*

"Be careful what you ask for," today's
sermon, cloaked. You may wish, after all,
that the Indians had more consistently
wiped out whole colonies. Jamestown,

I ask you: why did the black dog mournfully
step out before the truck's bright glory?
To make me cry? Which came first—the median
or the mastery? Do we see crosses impaling the blue
hillside or are those telephone poles?
"Do we 'see,'" to paraphrase, "telephone poles?"

Conflict resolution.
I have a complicated reaction because
I do not have an interest
in direction. You're driving along
on a highway, a bump
on a log in this river
we are in this life:

Murfreesboro.
The initiate is unafraid
of the covenant. It makes me think (of)
(instead of reminding me) of
the pure diorama (of)
the daily huge.
In place. A common complaint: I'm high
up above and I can't get down

to it.

Portrait

The thing to avoid is in that frame,
the reasoned screen fixing light
and shade in pithy squares of shape.
A man sitting outside in a wood chair,
his shirt is brighter than the page
he squints at. The book has browned,
like skin, with exposure. There is
the indispensable one. If
it is this easy to paint

objects why not call it
"portraiture"? The hunch
of shoulder, the magnet
of the subject at the center, hedged
around with frets and greenery.
Diminishing and cantilevered
(staying out of my way)
on the gentle slope. Leaving,
when he comes indoors
for respite, a charred spot.

I have changed the wrong thing.
The pang of fixity, a bleached
and empty rocker. If he will burn
so resolutely in a fraction
of the doorway, in the cool hewing
of the garden, then why not call it
martyrdom?

A Syllogism

One is one too many, pathos
being the domain of the rhetorician.
"My heart is broken . . . ;" and with uncommon
clarity you see it's what everyone else
is feeling all the time. A sweeping
generalization, a few, but
nevertheless. If feeling were accessible
then would we need scales,
and monitors, to help arrange, to orchestrate,
our daily action? *I have*
finally given up on you.

Action, guided by feeling, is the assumption
of our progress along the concourse.
How could I—or, optimistically, how *can* I
move to convince you of the single
absolute? Words being
the fracture of genesis. We learn
by doing: softly speaking
for romantic apprehension, the heroic
process of succor turns to battle
when we introduce such armies
as responded to our call for mercenaries.
I needed to kiss someone.

And "furthermore"
keeps visiting my rest. Action,
dictated by feeling, now that's
something else again—
dictated by feeling, action is something else
altogether, made righteous
by the gentle approbation that we sense
in our society for such concert,
if you will but pause a moment
before stressing that particular item
it will gain you countless
points. The panelists flaunt
their numeral cards, high in the air
over their hot heads
and ours. *No one*
has ever loved anybody.

Out of Town

1. We are approaching a mountain,
    fording a stream,
    bedazzled by the rotten little town.
    The certain sights one cannot see
    walking with us: your black birds
    changing place in the simple field.
    All on the rim of useful space.
    The complete town growing old upstate.

2. We approach the mountain for months,
    caressing the backsides of old houses
    in which God has made the men begin to bald
    and the men have taken action to reverse it.
    Corduroy sheathing hyperactive thighs . . . Bingo!
    Possible sweethearts bedeck the long tables.

3. We approach the mountain painstakingly
    in paved deliberation. Its peak
    is blind to junkets, its whole displacement
    remains to be seen. We set off
    with the previous world on our backs,
    grateful for vision to fix our sight:
    to concentrate on the slow-going
    is to survive the channel-crossing and the nullifying
    struggle for constancy. We cause
    the depletion of a huge distance,
    sugarcoating the blue mountain,
    and on those days we travel at the pace of realism,
    we contemplate anachronism.

Day Laborers

On the construction site
            orange cones, a black
foundation poured on
            the very void

we've been ignoring. Who is doing the pouring? I've been
            wearing a lot
of white lately, and I have risked my life for this projection—
            up on a ladder, high
above the contract, contracting—
            a progression into the zone of futures

in a ditch by the side of the interstate
            with a pointed
stick wearing the vaporous fluorescent bib of an arbiter
            you carry the bag of open spaces

as in Job's showcase rendition
            we must not even formulate the question
Don't you like to use the last
of something before you use the first
of something new? The contractions get closer and closer
            together; *well I do too.*

You seek compensation
        for some grievous injury. And you've just
wasted another gesture. Hush, dogged impulse, I will strive
        to preserve your innocence, you function
as neither husband
        nor wife. You are the drone
of something redundant

But I guess one goes where one is called.
        And is lucky to have been culled
from the ignominious band of idols
        on the corner, unregistered,
waiting for owners to drive by
        and pluck filler for the niche.
On all fours, face to the bottom
        of asphalt, breathing in such hot perfume as rises
from lava. Supervising a giant
        claw. Panting like a god
in the afterglow of the newly minted.

Press Play

In your truck without a notion, fighting a lot of feeling
with a huge supply of answers, we are listeners.

By this dim lighting that we sometimes find disquieting
songs play, stiff vocal support for common
tears, *tears* rising fast
and falling down like the dysfunctional word it is.

Turn my cheek to you: fuzz, deflected angle. You see me.
My face toward you I see you, the gauzy lens of you.

Messenger, decrease the pressure of the song on me.

Lie down with me. It can't be that I don't love you.
Every second rocketing, summoned.
What will we have once our songs
are relegated to their place? *A rise*

in the level of substandard expectancy,
a fluttering without correction in the ear
of the candidate, an indigenous people gone
delinquent, marginalized.

You must guess and guess again. Terrible waters
break over my head. I hum opportunistically,
fantasizing several eventualities. We speak less, we
kiss and kiss until the kiss
falls meaningless.

The Devil in Massachusetts

At last, an apple a day. Now
we can begin, colonial villagers,
our recreation, fanning out into the negative
spaces of this compound. Every stand of trees a haven
for the motif of the tall, severe
minister. The Black Man
who has never acted against us so much
as against nature: when he makes his move
across the macro-board from east to west the afflicted
parties (riddled with "angry" sores, self-described) must howl
as if affronted in their bosom and moonwalk spastically
across the wide pine boards in the direction of Mecca, ungodly
onions pointing heavenward.

Backwards he travels against historical
expediency, eschewing dreams so real they taste of mother
lodes and free love. Leaving behind seedless grapes and scaly
avocados he crosses a desert of illusion
to reforge the mouth-watering pass where snow barely
melts, back, back past plains
and unimpeded wind, to where endurance is a buzzword and the money
smells like molasses from Barbados,
where lobsters crawl onto the succoring shore like cockroaches
tasting sugar on a counterculture, giant
instruments of cold salience. I cannot think of a better
time to end our pointless globe-trotting,
when all is said and done and the Word backwards is still flesh
and we have never looked better than we do now
in our period garb.

Distinguished Reunion

I took a walk across the top
of the dunes. The wind runs contrary
to your expectations: I was not alone
on the ridge. I am never
alone. Crashing through
the undergrowth to emerge onto plains
of beach grass resembling
waves of grain, to my left there were vantages
offering the illusion
of an ocean, far below, extending directly

precipitously from the base
of said cataclysmic structure. Like a sheet of paper,
the water, far below, as though
there was no beach, no safety net, no strip of sand
running in place the width of our height and
an ocean's depth. I am never alone with
nothing to eat, no one
to play with, and nowhere
to run. Height is one perspective; I am now
as tall as I'll ever be. The ocean is a plate
of glass all registered by angry
motivations. It goes up and down and out in the general direction
of your head, full-grown companion, where
your crown caps the scrub pine,
where your loneliness and majesty are most absurd,
most deferred to.

Mister Pitiful: A Literary Biography

They say a billion images—
your entire life—flash before your eyes
when you die. They say this for a reason.
He went out for a walk in the woods on a snowy evening.

He saw a white bear hugging a tree
and it shocked him. Brought to mind all the loving
he had done—all gone wrong. *I can't help
this feeling. Trying to find a reason
to believe. Sock it to me.* Stop it for me.

Warm tones, a kind of plunking
guitar to counteract, even contradict, what first convinced
him about the act of love. This critical
approach to soul. *I never had school
(I am unschooled) but I've learned a lot and taught
it all to you.* We have invested
in a riot of perennials.

In the white woods he crunches steadily
along, drumming up doves from the brambles.
One hotel room after another containing
his flesh in the early years—and there
were no others. *It shot me through with longing, my eyes
trained on* . . . We get sick of the hyperbolic
elevations: at twenty-six he deserves to represent neither Cupid
on the rack nor the wedding band
on the hand of a blue-collar man. This was a walk

that would claim for silence
every little bunny and the endangered monarch.
While I can still articulate
you remember my sobs; those were uncalculated.
Seagulls en masse above the thawing lake
my agent says "we have a hit," Soul on Ice
straight to #1. The water's
surface under light is made to look
the way an orange peel would look, blue
like the peel of a blue orange
like blue orange peel. How do folks

survive this duality? *Pain in my heart*
And that's why I prefer, to friends, strangers.
Real love hangs over his slick shoulders as he attends
to the business of pleasuring. We are charged

with the riot of perennials
my stomach in knots waiting for the snow
which, when it fell, made the road
far less unmanageable than had been cautioned. Eternally

narrowly averted. The snow
snaking across in white
swaths, then, humorously, sidling

to cut sloppily in front of me. In due course a thaw will set in.
In the garden when you feed your breasts to me, Aretha.

Rowena swallows yr. nocturnal spooge

Emprison her soft hand, and let her rave
And feed deep, deep upon her peerless eyes!
—John Keats

Beginning with a fantasy of abuse,
a syrupy edition of nightfall. Was it for "this"? I.e.;
no archetypal character in this context,
the next day came a pure, washed-out
sensation. I had ghosted my love out of time.

      • • • • •

You, you're just the person I've been
waiting to talk to, gesture
wildly gesticulating.
Oh my lord, the balm of acquaintance:
and I fancy that in our unguarded moments
we react to each other like oil
does to water (and water to oil for that matter).

      • • • • •

It continues to be a soft and gentle *nacht*.
We are out in it. You have raped what you were supposed to love.
My Gosh I don't know how you're feeling
                  (dark shadow)
                      but I am filled with light.
The night sets in, over and over.

      • • • • •

begin at the beginning with a fantasy of nightfall,
an unbound edition of blue.
Take the word *permanent* and
apply it to this address with a grain of salt:
every imagined revelation,
every imaginable revelatory
rollicking dream of the perfect stranger,
dumb weight in her arms,
laboring under the impression . . .

. . . . .

Gosh the river's so pretty
I have no idea who I am.
It's based on angles, a slant of perception.
I feel a jerk.
A golden-haired arm
carving a niche in which for me
to stick it to me.
It says in the gospel you have to find someone
who won't let you go. In my neat pinafore

. . . . .

maybe I'll never . . .

. . . . .

I'll never.
(scooped it up too often in the dark of night.)

Chinatown, Oh

It all goes down at the Grand Hotel
in Lisboa . . . Chicago . . . Glasgow. None of these exactly
rhyme. Traipsing charlatans and clairvoyant
prostitutes and makeup artists, in residence.

In the taste test I identify correctly
with all the leading character
actors. At the screening we rose mightily
to the occasion. The samples

are more addictive than the product itself. *I'm free,*
I thought, *free at last,* whirling in the small room,
washing my hands of the sticky stuff
with sweet-smelling soap from a plastic dispenser.

I have fun with you in the mental landscape.
"I never expected to feel this way," coming
from my side of the table. "Do you kiss
your mother with that mouth?"

Suddenly it gets crowded in here—
there is too much to share.
Slavishly I am paying you
all the little attentions

—*my mother*   my brother   *my mother*
my lover   *my brother*   my mother—
slap   slap   slap.
Imagination has never been a friend to me:

in the early days
I would climb up a hill and climb
up into your bed. You are not there
or you are; the feat is in keeping my eyes

shut and pressing
processing my face against the appropriate
surface: your absence or your presence.
This can't be heterosexuality . . .

this must be heterosexuality.
I've turned into somebody else already.
It's just like the difference between dream and reality,
Mrs. Claus. Methodically,

I don't understand how my body
will go down this tangled hill of dune:
feet first, sand scrambled, marbleized
like fancy stationery. Pretty stones,

within reach; an arm's length, a Wild Tiger Story,
a long, tall candle appropriated
piece-meal in its whole-cloth, wrought-iron protestation
of a candle-stick holder from a retail dream, one in which an iambic

street is rhymed syllabically with "cantering."
He speaks to me when I am asleep
so that I will not remonstrate,
every behavior modeled by our flesh. See

if it calls forth in you an answering
vocation: you may find yourself relieved at the platonic
bed-warmer, the fraternal surprise visit in the top-bunk
of the double-decker. "Certain 'violations

of actual circumstances' (to borrow from Richard
Wilbur)." To borrow from
Anne Stevenson,
of *Bitter Fame*

fame. And
in his office the private dick told me I was an
"incomplete blinker"—he asked me to daydream a little bit
for him: public demonstration.

The Proverbial Handshake:
The Sharon Olds Poem

During intercourse, after orgasm, I recently discovered,
listening to the radio, the cervix contracts, deadly serious.
For conserving energy and time, to hold the sperm
closely into the bosom of the womb: to maximize
potentiality. This confirms my suspicion that we might be
fruitful. When I feel the purse strings, spasms
such as these, and your penis is still right there
in my vagina I grow proud of my body's brain and always mindful
that for you these little tugs—ringing proof
of what has come to pass between us and of what
direction all our work is going in—are also tight.
They're tighter and they're part of a continuum—
praise and acceptance, rejection and denial, perdition
and revelation, consecration and endorsement, not to mention
downright graciousness and hospitality—which extends
between us like a bridge between the mainland and the island
or like a handshake over a heavy oaken desktop. Only firmer.

Everything Demystified

On the long drive to Consummation
Gorge I am indulged. Thoughts of my life
ahead

on second viewing it flows like honey, the film-drenched
reel, technically colored. We laugh
at the sad parts, become aroused
in the soundless closed-up kiss. Laugh again
at the enactment of behavior. Is there a word
for *impeach* in every language?

On the way I am privileged
to put a whole new spin on deprivation
a critique of naive and degraded notions of referentiality
the more water you drink
you want more water

he said cruelly
I think I love—
the idea of you. Not intonation
but affect. If I had only known
there would be this many people I never
would have left home. *Oh country moan*

    . . . . .

Now it seems so exotic to go North,
forever witty, forever urbane,
forever ascending a scale of dance instruction,
all aghast at the misdirections
on the back of the box.

Not just a nautical theme but a going concern:
tremendous anchor effective
rusted into the ground, the grassy yard
going green
against brown. And that is my hometown,
not some pathology of reduction. Everyone says
"nightmare of suburbia" smugly

and is understood. The not-insignificant pond
being so blue as to reflect
the sky grown over with green,

benign by nature
resting just on the outside
of all the rustic, all the flagrant sceptres
and cameos of the flesh, the air
of a soft summer day

in my youth, so free of coy evasion, so easily recaptured
from the bare arms of mystery.
And stuffed full of things nonreflective.

Farewell O land of the festooned
armadillo, the albatross of contumely, the torments
of July. One way of life is ended; it's a big
change to explain and it's hard not to be boring.

The Sun in Winter

Late afternoon the starving light
denudes a neighbor's tree, transfers
dear property to flame, casts
gold all in his painterly face.
Simple description accomplishing
devotion; a call for motives
interior, dynastic.

One seat offers one vantage.
The window is adored for its demented
optimism—and with unguarded premonition
tells the patron
how much dark will cloud
an issue, and how the shortened span
makes certain curses come like blessings
on the head of days alluded to as "dying."
A less occluded view might queer this open
invitation to the static atmosphere: *Come
and stay.*

Oh, stay the sun
and make some meager homily
fixed on ginger-red wood siding
to reflect into the eye
a burnished spasm of glad
tiding: antidote to venom of our imagery's
declining.

It all ends in resignation

I

If you, yourself a gentleman
farmer, had the same ecstatic dream—a house—
each night, wouldn't it tell you something
about impending dawn,
about how you might wish to fritter away
the day, the balance of your inheritance,
such slender means?

II

Consistently the ideal
of a commune, or even of communal projects—
or just cooperation, for that matter—
has collapsed under its stresses:
endless board meetings,
the pressing need, the exigency
of leadership. A godhead
is lacking from our blueprint,
our proposal for the screenplay, the project,
our finest hour.

III

Waking up in the house the morning after
all renovations have been made:
Nothing lost.
The long narrow providential window still looks hungrily
on extenuating rows of cotton,
planted right for generations,
all correct in perspectival
and genetic confluence.

IV

Hammer away, boys,
hammer away, you cannot wake me
to the dawning light
when I have spent all evening
making meals for the deserving.

V

When I have made a habit of combining
found ingredients. When I
have finally chosen
from among you those

who dare to make this leap
from faint schematic—
such daffy venture
as to make a moneylender
run screaming
in laughter, in terror

VI

—to a body.

Healing Song for the Inner Ear
Michael S. Harper (1984)

The Passion of the Right-Angled Man
T. R. Hummer (1984)

Dear John, Dear Coltrane
Michael S. Harper (1985)

Poems from the Sangamon
John Knoepfle (1985)

In It
Stephen Berg (1986)

The Ghosts of Who We Were
Phyllis Thompson (1986)

Moon in a Mason Jar
Robert Wrigley (1986)

Lower-Class Heresy
T. R. Hummer (1987)

Poems: New and Selected
Frederick Morgan (1987)

Furnace Harbor: A Rhapsody of
  the North Country
Philip D. Church (1988)

Bad Girl, with Hawk
Nance Van Winckel (1988)

Blue Tango
Michael Van Walleghen (1989)

Eden
Dennis Schmitz (1989)

Waiting for Poppa at the Smithtown
  Diner
Peter Serchuk (1990)

Great Blue
Brendan Galvin (1990)

What My Father Believed
Robert Wrigley (1991)

Something Grazes Our Hair
S. J. Marks (1991)

Walking the Blind Dog
G. E. Murray (1992)

The Sawdust War
Jim Barnes (1992)

The God of Indeterminacy
Sandra McPherson (1993)

Off-Season at the Edge of the World
Debora Greger (1994)

Counting the Black Angels
Len Roberts (1994)

Oblivion
Stephen Berg (1995)

To Us, All Flowers Are Roses
Lorna Goodison (1995)

Honorable Amendments
Michael S. Harper (1995)

Points of Departure
Miller Williams (1995)

Dance Script with Electric Ballerina
Alice Fulton (reissue, 1996)

To the Bone: New and Selected Poems
Sydney Lea (1996)

Floating on Solitude
Dave Smith (3-volume reissue, 1996)

Bruised Paradise
Kevin Stein (1996)

Walt Whitman Bathing
David Wagoner (1996)

Rough Cut
Thomas Swiss (1997)

Paris
Jim Barnes (1997)

The Ways We Touch
Miller Williams (1997)

The Rooster Mask
Henry Hart (1998)

The Trouble-Making Finch
Len Roberts (1998)

Grazing
Ira Sadoff (1998)

Turn Thanks
Lorna Goodison (1999)

Traveling Light:
    Collected and New Poems
David Wagoner (1999)

Some Jazz a While:
    Collected Poems
Miller Williams (1999)

The Iron City
John Bensko (2000)

Songlines in Michaeltree:
    New and Collected Poems
Michael S. Harper (2000)

Pursuit of a Wound
Sydney Lea (2000)

The Pebble: Old and New Poems
Mairi MacInnes (2000)

Chance Ransom
Kevin Stein (2000)

House of Poured-Out Waters
Jane Mead (2001)

The Silent Singer:
    New and Selected Poems
Len Roberts (2001)

The Salt Hour
J. P. White (2001)

NATIONAL POETRY SERIES

Eroding Witness
Nathaniel Mackey (1985)
Selected by Michael S. Harper

Palladium
Alice Fulton (1986)
Selected by Mark Strand

Cities in Motion
Sylvia Moss (1987)
Selected by Derek Walcott

The Hand of God and a Few
    Bright Flowers
William Olsen (1988)
Selected by David Wagoner

The Great Bird of Love
Paul Zimmer (1989)
Selected by William Stafford

Stubborn
Roland Flint (1990)
Selected by Dave Smith

The Surface
Laura Mullen (1991)
Selected by C. K. Williams

The Dig
Lynn Emanuel (1992)
Selected by Gerald Stern

My Alexandria
Mark Doty (1993)
Selected by Philip Levine

The High Road to Taos
Martin Edmunds (1994)
Selected by Donald Hall

Theater of Animals
Samn Stockwell (1995)
Selected by Louise Glück

The Broken World
Marcus Cafagña (1996)
Selected by Yusef Komunyakaa

Nine Skies
A. V. Christie (1997)
Selected by Sandra McPherson

Lost Wax
Heather Ramsdell (1998)
Selected by James Tate

So Often the Pitcher Goes to Water
   until It Breaks
Rigoberto González (1999)
Selected by Ai

Renunciation
Corey Marks (2000)
Selected by Philip Levine

Manderley
Rebecca Wolff (2001)
Selected by Robert Pinsky

OTHER POETRY VOLUMES

Local Men and *Domains*
James Whitehead (1987)

Her Soul beneath the Bone: Women's
   Poetry on Breast Cancer
Edited by Leatrice Lifshitz (1988)

Days from a Dream Almanac
Dennis Tedlock (1990)

Working Classics: Poems on Industrial
   Life
Edited by Peter Oresick and Nicholas Coles
(1990)

Hummers, Knucklers, and Slow Curves:
   Contemporary Baseball Poems
Edited by Don Johnson (1991)

The Double Reckoning of Christopher
   Columbus
Barbara Helfgott Hyett (1992)

Selected Poems
Jean Garrigue (1992)

New and Selected Poems, 1962–92
Laurence Lieberman (1993)

The Dig and *Hotel Fiesta*
Lynn Emanuel (1994)

For a Living: The Poetry of Work
Edited by Nicholas Coles and Peter Oresick
(1995)

The Tracks We Leave: Poems on
Endangered Wildlife of North
   America
Barbara Helfgott Hyett (1996)

Peasants Wake for Fellini's *Casanova* and
   Other Poems
Andrea Zanzotto; edited and translated by
John P. Welle and Ruth Feldman; drawings
by Federico Fellini and Augusto Murer
(1997)

Moon in a Mason Jar and *What My*
   Father Believed
Robert Wrigley (1997)

The Wild Card: Selected Poems,
   Early and Late
Karl Shapiro; edited by Stanley Kunitz and
   David Ignatow (1998)

Turtle, Swan and *Bethlehem in*
   Broad Daylight
Mark Doty (2000)

Illinois Voices: An Anthology of
   Twentieth-Century Poetry
Edited by Kevin Stein and G. E. Murray
(2001)

University of Illinois Press
1325 South Oak Street
Champaign, IL 61820–6903
www.press.uillinois.edu